This book
belongs to:

may your christmas
be merry and bright

Peace on Earth

Seas and Greetings.

FROM: SANTA

Peace on Earth

TO:
FROM:

SURPRISE

NAUGHTY

MERRY CHRISTMAS

THE NIGHT BEFORE Christmas

JOY

Thank you for purchasing this coloring book, one of many in the Chubby Mermaid series. Please don't forget to sign into Amzon.com – Deborah Muller Coloring Books and leave a review.

Follow me on Facebook
Chubby Mermaid Art by Deborah Muller

Join my Coloring Group on Facebook
Deborah Muller's Coloring Group

Instagram
Chubby Mermaid Art

Etsy
Chubby Mermaid

Pinterest
Deborah Muller Chubby Mermaid Art

Email
Chubbymermaid@hotmail.com

Website
ChubbyMermaidArt.com

Made in the USA
Monee, IL
16 December 2020

53390452R00039